MODERN
medi-tation

COLORING FOR FOCUS AND CREATIVITY

DR STAN RODSKI B.Ec., D.Sc.(BIO)
PEAK PERFORMANCE NEUROSCIENTIST

hardie grant books

About the Authors

Dr Stan Rodski B.Ec., D.Sc.(BIO)
Neuroscientist

Stan is a neuroscientist with over 30 years experience. He obtained his bachelors degree and qualified as a psychologist in 1985; in 1994, Stan completed his doctorate in Bio Science.

He is particularly interested in brain performance and the impact of stress on performance levels. Currently, he is involved in neuroscientific research on stress coping mechanisms in our personal, family and work life.

Stan has worked in private practice in Australia and internationally, coaching individuals, elite sporting teams and many Australian and international Top 500 companies.

Most recently, he has been applying brain science research to areas such as improved sleep, fatigue and stress, and energy revitalization and management.

This research has led to a number of programs that Stan facilitates all over the world. The coloring book series was initially available through these programs where its success in creating a calming effect was first recognized and established.

Jack Dowling

Jack is an architecture student at RMIT University in Melbourne, Australia; co-director of online art community, Artselect; and illustrator for the adult coloring series of books. Jack describes finding patterns as a creative and iterative process. He hopes readers will similarly apply their own creative intuition, allowing the mind to relax and enjoy the meditative qualities that come from these exercises.

CONTENTS

Introduction

Welcome to *Medi*-tation, a coloring book for adults based on brain science.

In this third book in our series we will be focusing on three areas of brain activity that enable us to not only deal with stress better, but to also improve our performance from both a health and work perspective.

The brain amounts to only 2% of our body mass, but it uses 20% of our available energy to function well. Of these 20%, 80% is used subconsciously to complete the myriad vital tasks that our body needs to keep functioning. The remaining 20% is discretionary – available to us in our conscious world to think and do the things that come to mind.

It is a very delicate balance, involving the message pathways controlled by our brain using chemical and electrical signals. Neuroscience monitors these signals using various technologies to understand what is happening. For example, when we are alert and awake our brainwaves speed up from 14 to 30 cycles per second. This is called the beta state. When we are in deep sleep, our brainwaves slow down to 0.5 to 3.5 cycles per second, this is called the delta state; when we are in a sleepy state, our brainwaves move to 4 to 7 cycles per second, which is called theta state. Finally, when we are relaxing, our brain moves into alpha waves, which oscillate at 8 to 13 cycles per second.

In this book, we look at how coloring can have an impact on three of these states and more importantly how each can be improved. The book covers:

- **Alpha brain training** to achieve better relaxation; using coloring while listening to alpha wave sound

- **Beta brain training** to achieve better thinking; using coloring first, followed by brain stimulating beta wave exercises

- **Theta brain training** to achieve deep relaxation and better sleep; using coloring and stimulating the senses to impact the theta waves in the brain.

The coloring pages in this new book continue with designs especially created to engage the brain through repetition, pattern and control.

Let yourself go, and watch the creativity from your color and position choices come out of the page.

Have fun, stay calm and be creative.

Dr Stan Rodski – Neuroscientist

PART ONE
Healthy brain: coloring plus sound

THE PERFECT NUTRITION AND CONDIMENT FOR A RELAXED BRAIN

ACHIEVING BETTER RELAXATION THROUGH COLORING WHILE LISTENING TO ALPHA WAVE STIMULATING MUSIC IS LIKE HEALTHY FOOD PLUS YOUR FAVOURITE CONDIMENT.

WHEN WE ARE TRYING TO RELAX WHILE COLORING, SOME OF US FIND QUIET ABSOLUTELY ESSENTIAL. NOISE OF ANY KIND IS EXPERIENCED AS DISTRACTING AND ANNOYING. FOR OTHERS, THE 'SOUNDS OF SILENCE' ARE EQUALLY DISTRACTING, AS OUR BRAIN SEARCHES FOR ANY DIVERSION IT CAN.

IN BOTH CASES, CERTAIN SOUNDS CAN HAVE A MAJOR EFFECT ON DEEPENING THE RELAXATION STATE THAT WE ARE SEEKING TO ACHIEVE WHILE COLORING.

LET'S LOOK AT THIS MORE CLOSELY

OUR BRAIN MOVES THROUGH A NUMBER OF BRAINWAVE STATES DURING OUR 24 HOUR SLEEP-WAKE CYCLE.

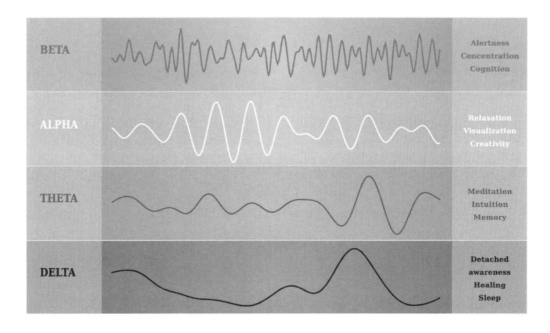

The alpha brainwave is associated with mental and physical relaxation. Produced by our brain, these waves oscillate (go up and down through a complete wave) 8 to 13 pulses per second. This is the brain's relaxed state — the state we need to achieve before we move into sleep. It is also the state we need to enter into as frequently as possible when awake to ensure we maintain our best brain performance: 'you can't have the accelerator on all the time or you will burn out the engine'.

This alpha state is automatically engaged for many of us when we color. But we can create an even deeper or more consistent relaxed state if we also listen to certain types of sound. Many studies have shown that sound in the form of music can have a significant impact on the brainwaves in the frontal cortex (above your eyes), causing the brainwaves to move into an alpha wave pattern. Some music/sound can make us feel relaxed (a harp), while other music/sound can do the reverse and cause us to be 'up beat' (drums).

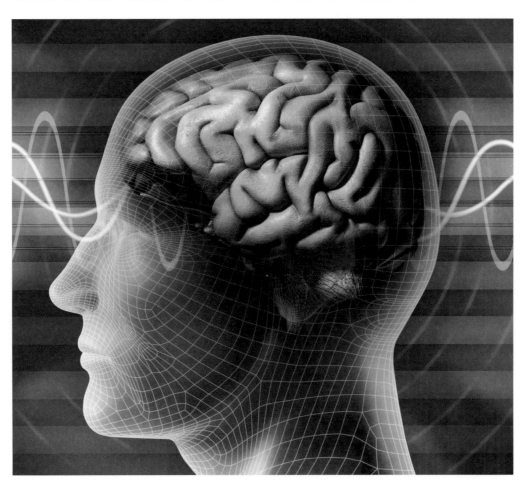

With the adult coloring technique, coloring pages have been designed to engage the brain in its favorite cognitive nutrition (brain food) of repetition, pattern and control (coloring between the lines). To keep the brain food analogy going, we can now add some 'spice' through music. While classical music has a profound impact on producing alpha waves, other music (depending on taste) can also at the very least help us shut out noise or remove quiet so that our brain can truly relax.

Neuroscience research into sound has found that sounds which lack loud-to-soft transitions, have smooth rythms, and create low arousal through a small range of notes with complimentary harmonies are immensely powerful in creating feelings of peace, contentment and relaxation.

We have developed ALPHAsounds© to meet these brain requirements for a great relaxation effect. The ALPHAsounds© can be downloaded from HTTPS://SOUNDCLOUD.COM/COLOURTATION

When you color using this book, try listening to these sounds (each piece lasts for 6 minutes).

SO LET'S GET STARTED

Go 'offline'(stop what you are doing) and color until the sounds stop, two or three times a day. You will observe how you have become more motivated, focused and able to problem-solve when you turn your mind back to the tasks of your day.

BE IN
THE MOMENT

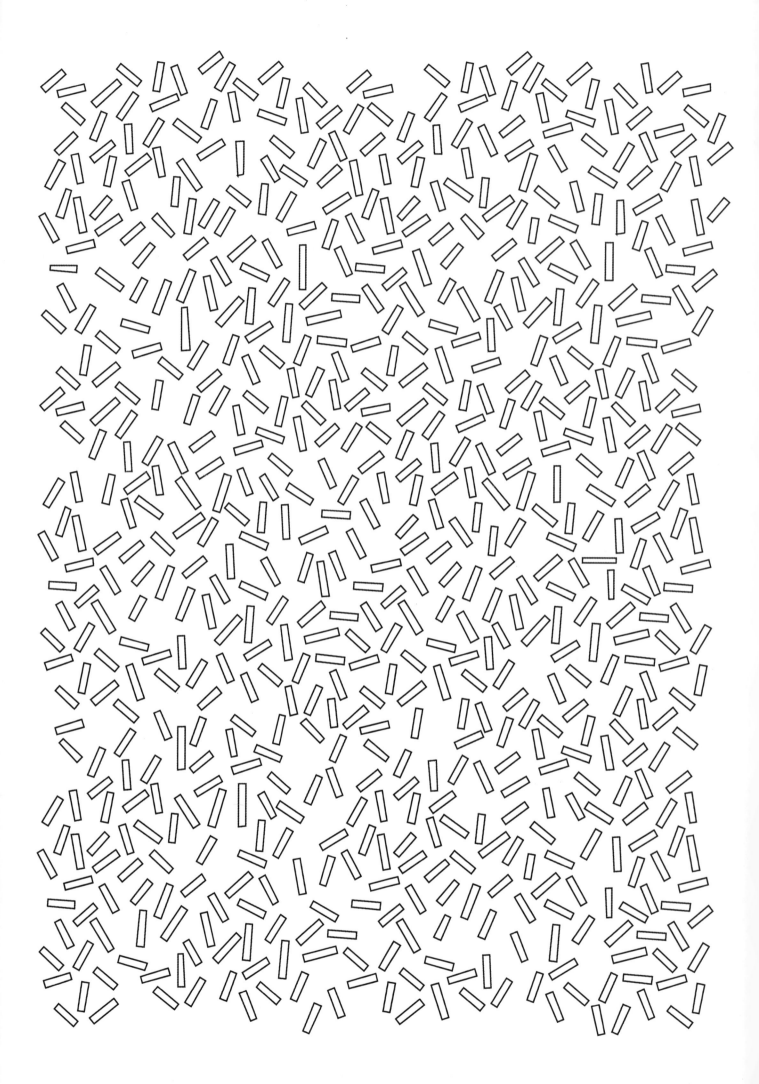

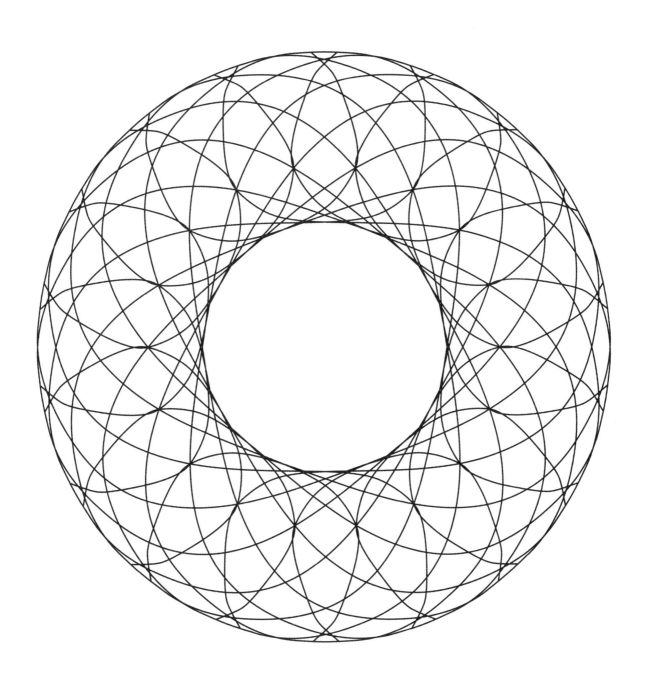

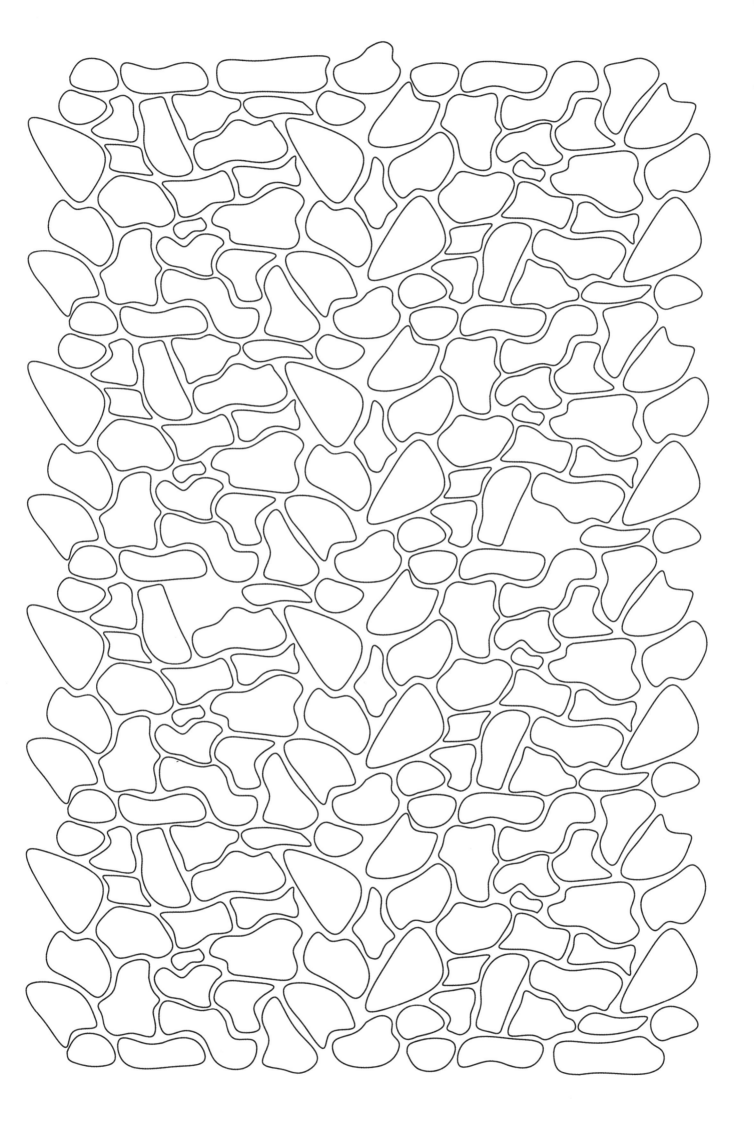

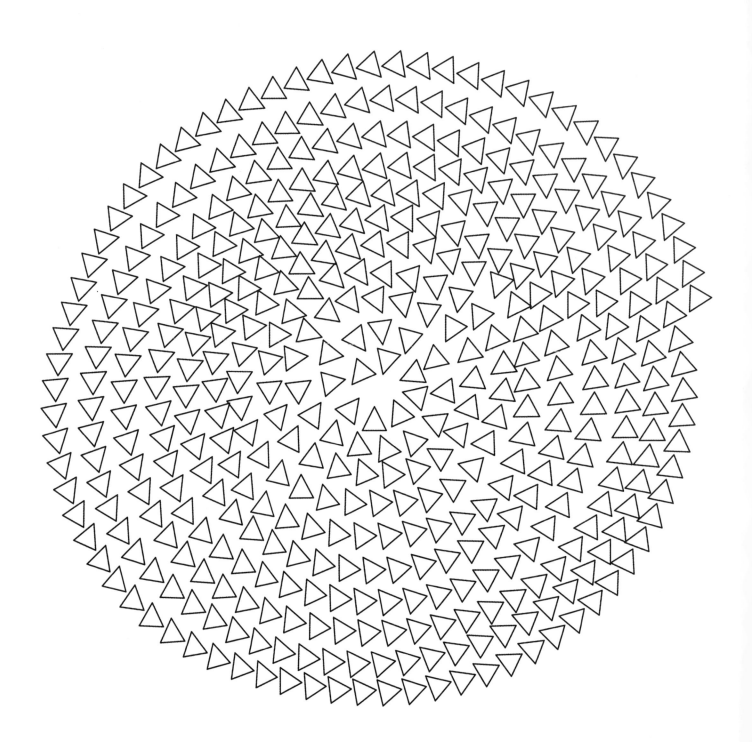

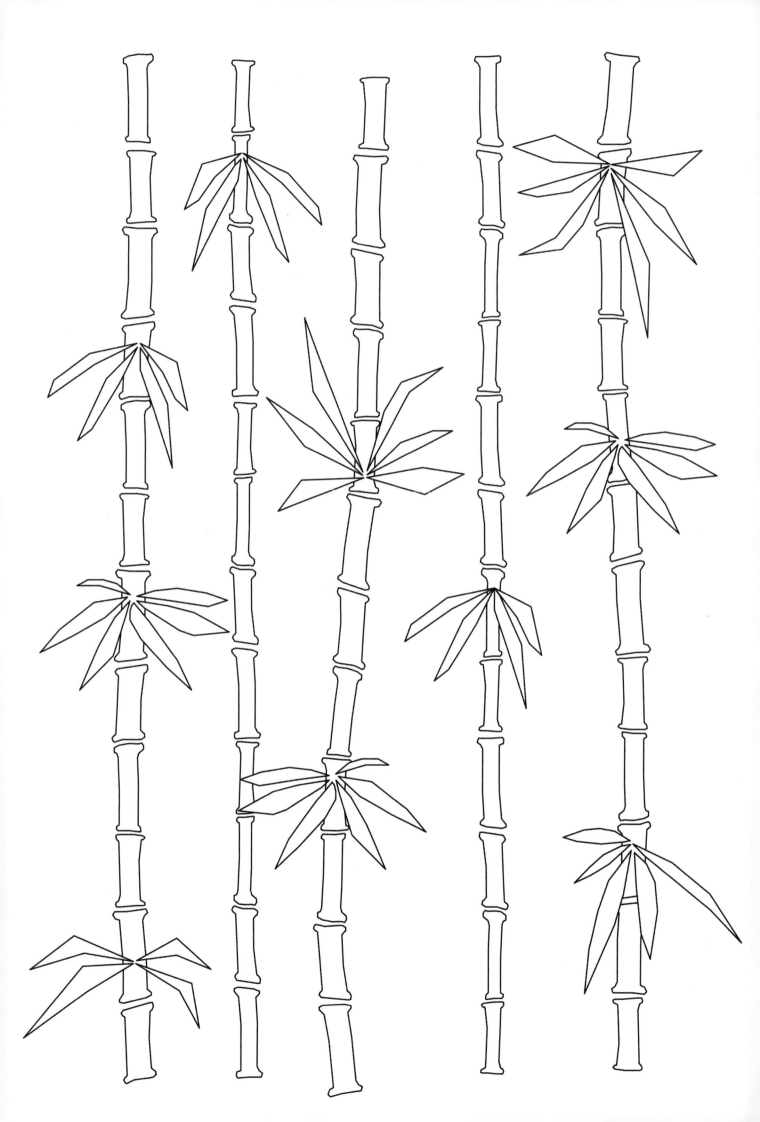

PART TWO
Better Brain Performance

THE ONE-TWO COMBINATION

COLORING AND THEN PRACTICING BRAIN STIMULATING BETA WAVE EXERCISES IS A GREAT COMBINATION TO IMPROVE BRAIN PERFORMANCE.

WHILE PREVIOUSLY, OUR FOCUS HAS BEEN ON RELAXING THE BRAIN, WE ALSO NEED TO CONSIDER HOW BEST TO IMPROVE ITS PERFORMANCE. SOMETIMES THE PROBLEM IS NOT THAT WE FEEL STRESSED, BUT RATHER THAT WE FEEL UNABLE TO 'GET GOING' OR LACK THE MOTIVATION TO DO SO. OUR BRAIN HAS PUT DOWN THE TOOLS, TO FORCE US TO STOP.

SO HOW DO WE GET GOING AGAIN, TO TACKLE THE 'I HAVE A JOB TO DO', 'KIDS TO PICK UP' AND 'A TENNIS GAME TO FINISH' SITUATIONS IN LIFE?

COLORING HAS A REAL ROLE TO PLAY HERE. IN THE NEUROSCIENCE OF PEAK PERFORMANCE, THE BRAIN AND ITS BRAINWAVE ACTIVITY ARE SEEN AS CRITICAL TO PEAK PERFORMANCE THINKING. WE NOW KNOW THAT THE PERFORMANCE OF OUR BRAIN IS ENHANCED WHEN WE APPROACH TASKS FROM A RELAXED STATE. WE ALL KNOW HOW HARD IT IS DO SOMETHING THAT HAS BEEN WORRYING US WITHOUT LET-UP. HOW MUCH BETTER TO GET ON WITH SOMETHING WHEN WE HAVEN'T THOUGHT ABOUT IT EXCESSIVELY BEFORE!

THIS IS WHAT THIS CHAPTER IS ABOUT: GETTING TO A BETTER BETA WAVE FROM A RELAXED ALPHA WAVE STATE. THE BETA WAVE PULSES AT 14 TO 30 PULSES PER SECOND AND IS GENERALLY GENERATED IN THE BRAIN'S LEFT HEMISPHERE.

Beta waves are integral in alertness and logical thinking. They also increase with social interaction, feelings of excitement and our goal orientation.

We will increase our ability to reach peak performance by combining our coloring (alpha wave) with neuro (brain) exercises to stimulate our beta waves.

EXERCISES TO STIMULATE BETA WAVES

(1) Get two pens (or pencils). With a pen in your usual writing hand, complete the image below on a sheet of paper.

Now swap the pen to your other hand and complete the image.

Finally, with a pen in each hand, complete the image at the same time. Try starting at different points on the image.

You are now stimulating both left and right hemispheres of your brain and are getting your brain ready to perform at its best.

(2) Hold up your left thumb and point your right index finger out as shown in the picture below.

Now fold your right hand index finger in and extend the right thumb up. At the same time, the other hand acts in reverse: extend your index finger and fold in your thumb. Remember, you can't have two fingers or two thumbs out or in at the same time.

Practice this to enable your brain to fire up and get ready for the tasks it needs to complete.

In this chapter, we are using brain stimulation exercises to prepare for the challenges of the day. Tasks will be far more effectively met if we come from a position of relaxation rather than already feeling burnt out.

Try this: color while listening to the music. But before jumping back into your tasks, try the two exercises above for a few minutes. Think of it as brain stretching exercises — you wouldn't run a marathon without first stretching your muscles to ensure you don't injure yourself!

See for yourself how your brain reacts to the stimulation, how it enables you to think more quickly and engage with those around you more effectively.

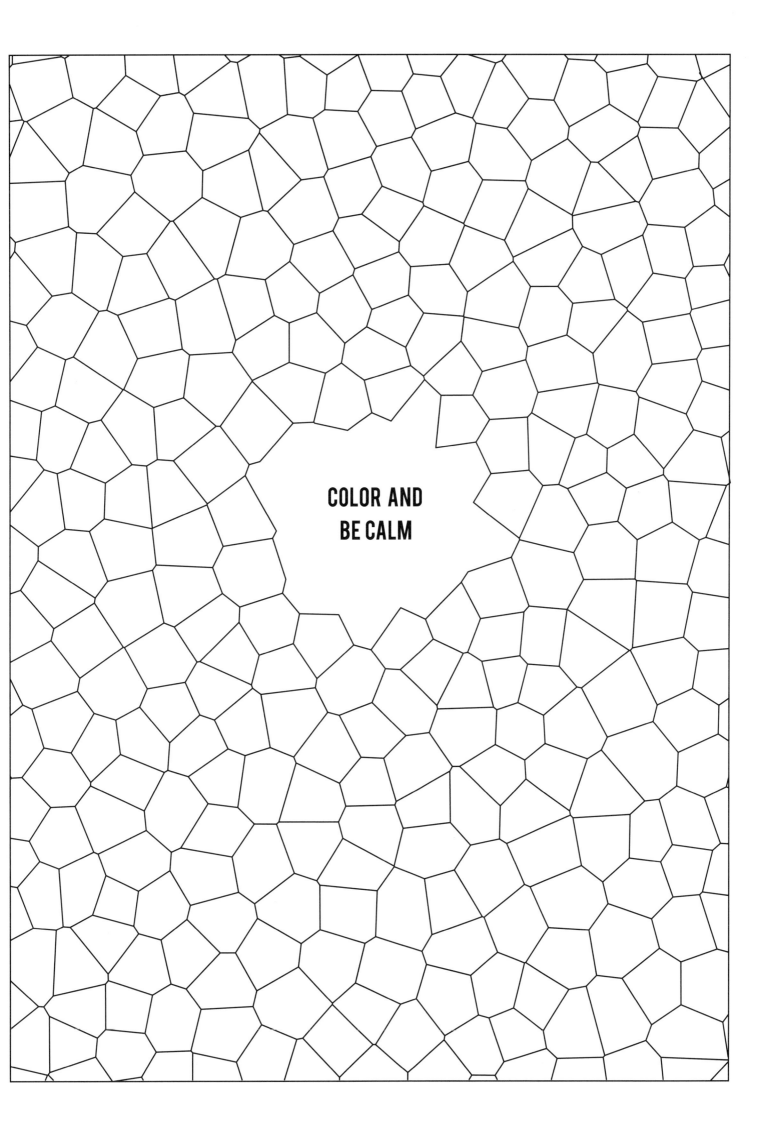

COLOR AND
BE CALM

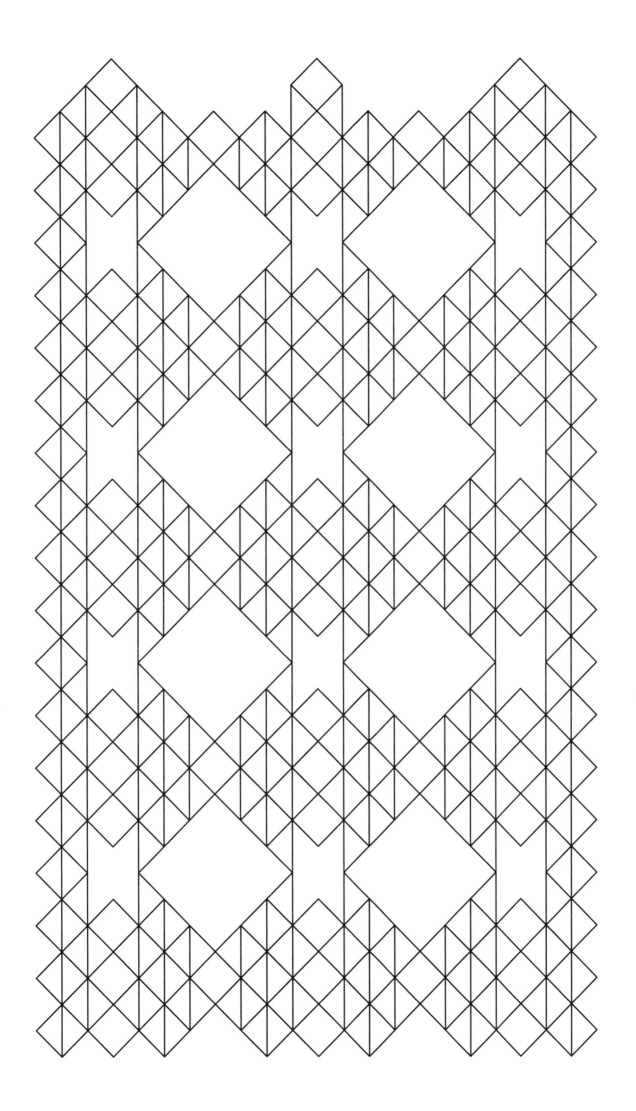

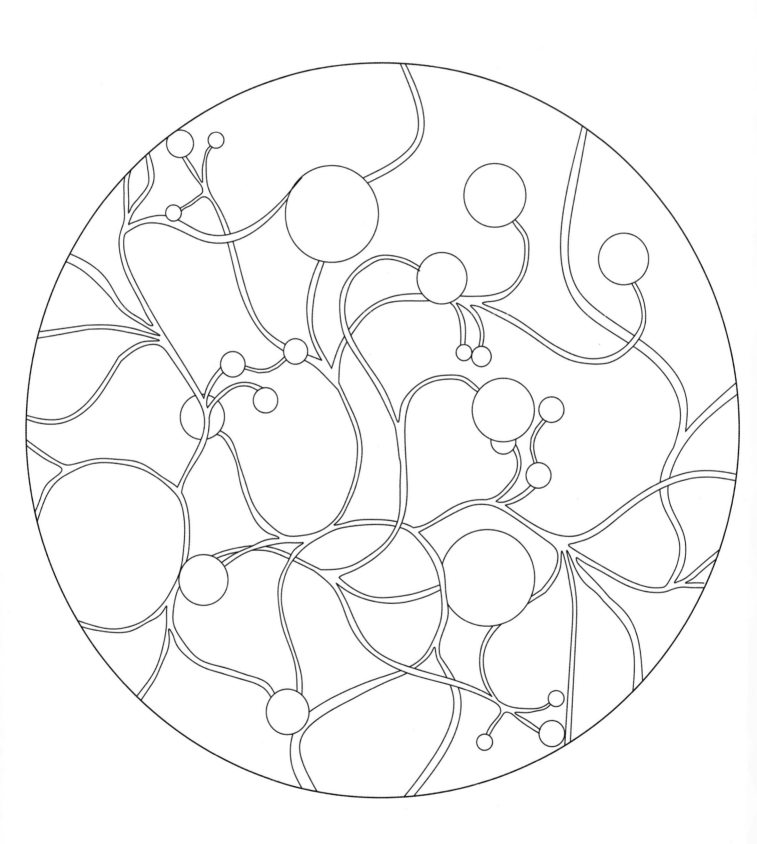

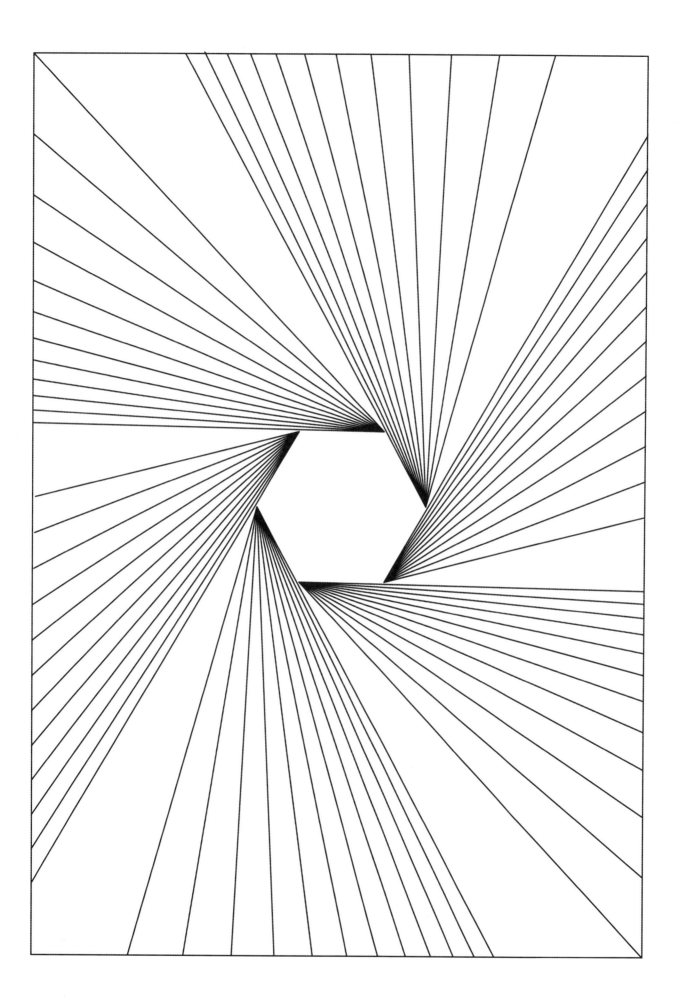

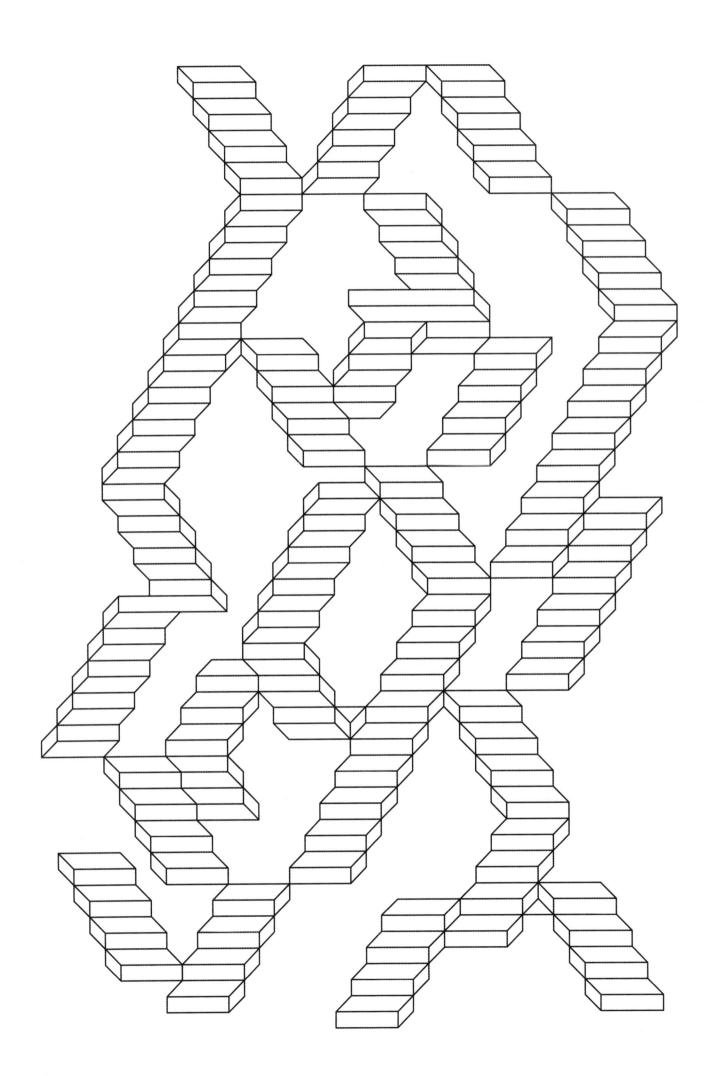

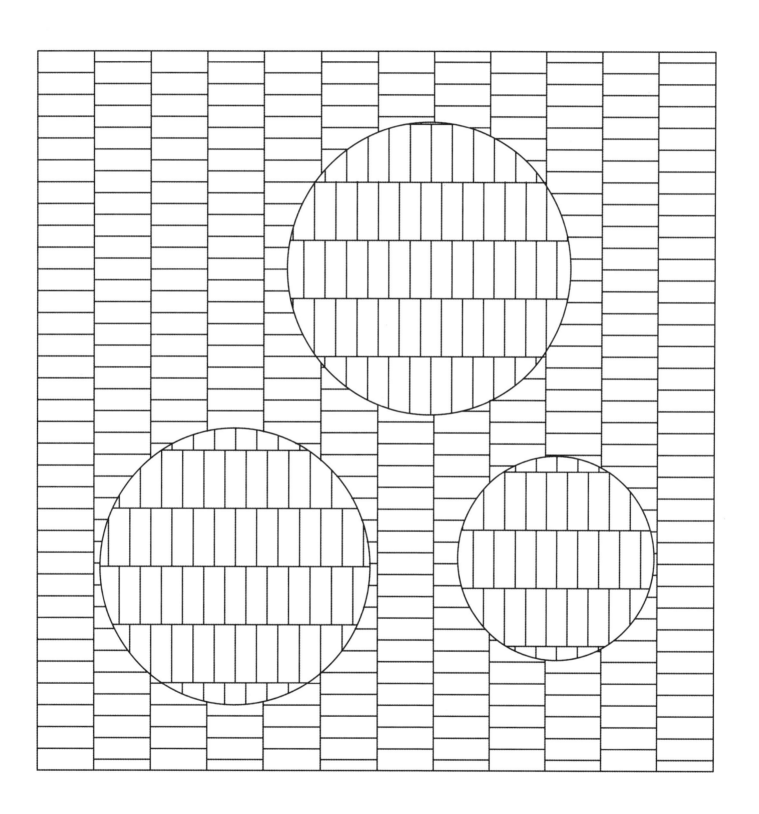

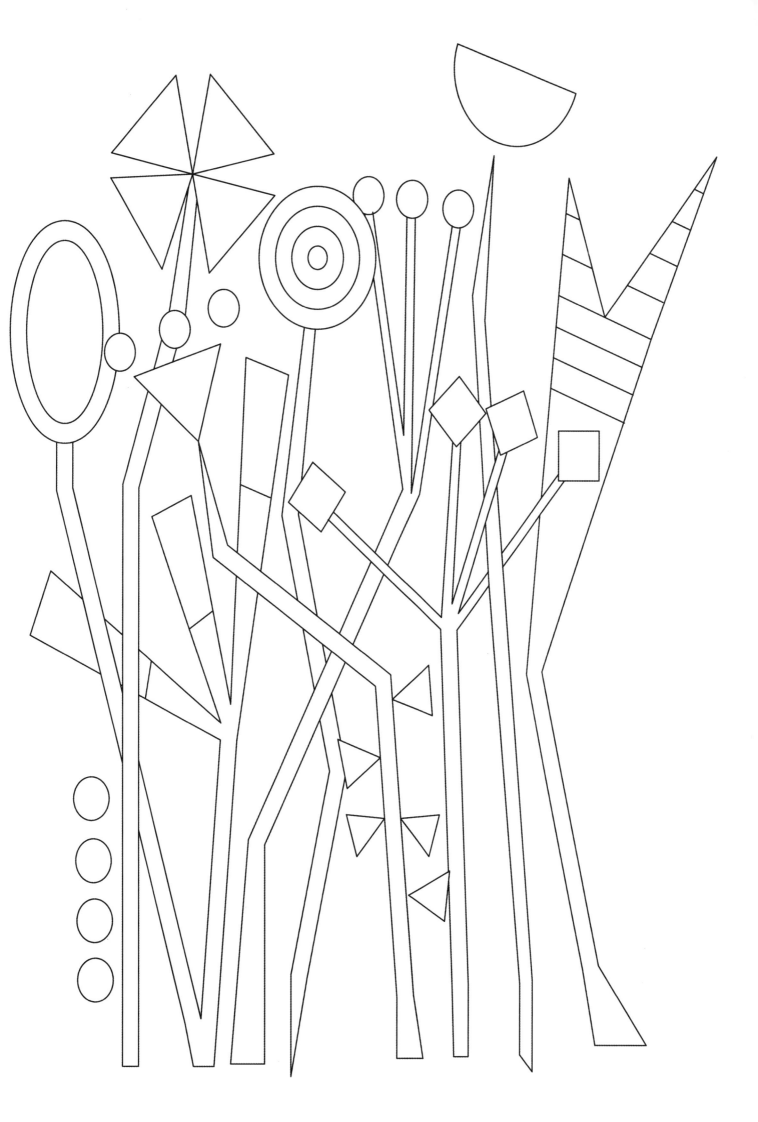

PART THREE

Better sleep and happiness

STIMULATING THE THETA BRAINWAVE

THE THETA BRAINWAVE IS PRODUCED COMMONLY WHEN WE ARE IN A STATE OF DEEP RELAXATION, OR WHEN WE ARE SLEEPY. THE BRAINWAVES SLOW DOWN TO BETWEEN 4 AND 7 WAVES PER SECOND.

THIS LEVEL OF BRAIN ACTIVITY IS OFTEN ASSOCIATED WITH OUR DEEP SEATED EMOTIONS AND SPIRITUALITY.
DURING THE THETA STAGE, THE BRAIN CAN BE LIKENED TO BEING IN A DEEPLY MEDITATIVE STATE.

BENEFITS THAT ARISE FOR THOSE WHO CAN ENTER A THETA STAGE THROUGH MEDITATION ARE WELL DOCUMENTED AND RESEARCHED. THE ISSUE IS THAT FOR MANY OF US, ACHIEVING THIS LEVEL OF RELAXATION IS DIFFICULT. THE MAIN REASONS FOR NOT TRYING THAT WE COME UP WITH ARE:

I DON'T HAVE TIME
I FORGET TO DO IT
I CAN'T STAY FOCUSED, SO WHY BOTHER?
I DON'T KNOW HOW TO DO IT RIGHT
THIS DOESN'T WORK FOR ME
I FALL ASLEEP
I FEEL SILLY DOING THIS & ITS BORING…

COLORING, COMBINED WITH ALPHAsounds©, CAN INDUCE A POWERFUL ALPHA STATE, BUT DOES NOT ACHIEVE A THETA

STATE. ENTERING INTO A THETA BRAINWAVE STATE, HOWEVER, CAN BE HIGHLY EFFECTIVE IN MAKING US FEEL HAPPY.

TO HELP US IN ACHIEVING A SENSE OF HAPPINESS, WE NEED TO ALSO STIMULATE THE OLFACTORY REGION OF THE BRAIN. THE OLFACTORY IS THE PART OF THE BRAIN THAT IS INVOLVED WITH THE SENSE OF SMELL.

SMELL, OR AROMA, HAS BEEN SHOWN TO HAVE A DRAMATIC IMPACT ON OUR FEELINGS AND ASSOCIATED BRAINWAVES. THE USE OF INCENSE IN VARIOUS RELIGIONS AND SPIRITUALITY PRACTICES IS WELL DOCUMENTED.

PEACEFULNESS AND CALMNESS COEXIST WITH OUR FEELINGS OF HAPPINESS. THE USE OF CALMING FRAGRANCES FROM CANDLES AND OILS OR SCENTED/INFUSED TEAS CAN GENERATE THESE FEELINGS FOR MANY OF US.

Neuroscience has shown that using calming or soothing aromas is particularly useful for the wind-down period of the day before bed.

Many of us suffer sleep deprivation — we just don't get enough sleep. The reasons are many, but can be summarized by our very busy world and schedules.

Using the method of coloring and listening to ALPHAsounds©, combined with stimulating the brain's theta waves through smell, can help you sleep — and good sleep is essential for maintaining your energy levels and brain functions every day.

So tonight, take in the aromas of a relaxing candle or relaxation tea, and color some of the images in this chapter of the book while listening to the ALPHAsounds©.

You will enjoy a blissful sleep and wake up refreshed and ready to have a happy and productive day.

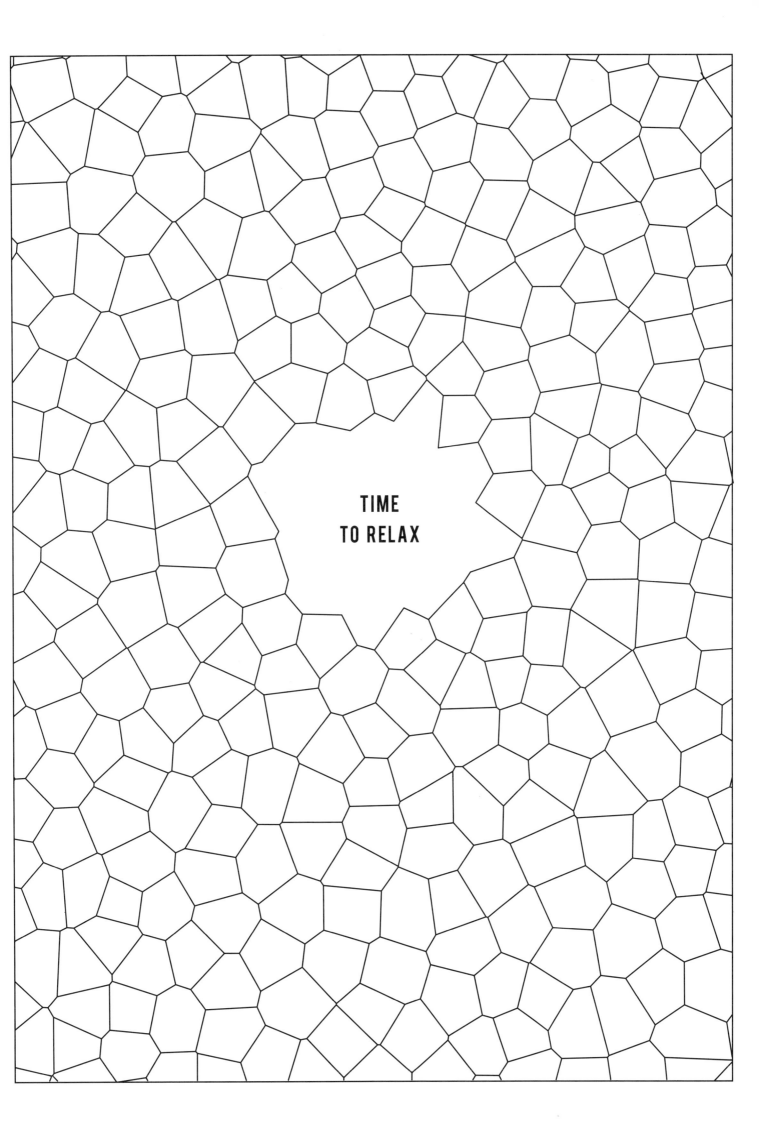

TIME
TO RELAX

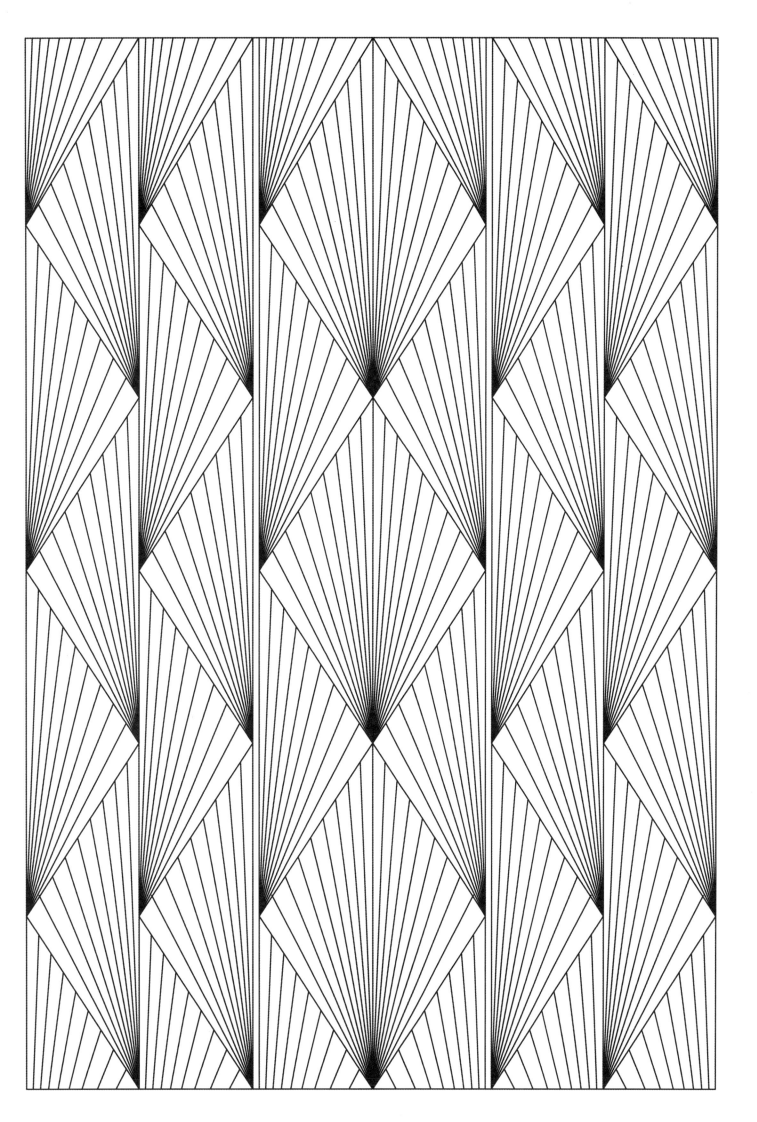

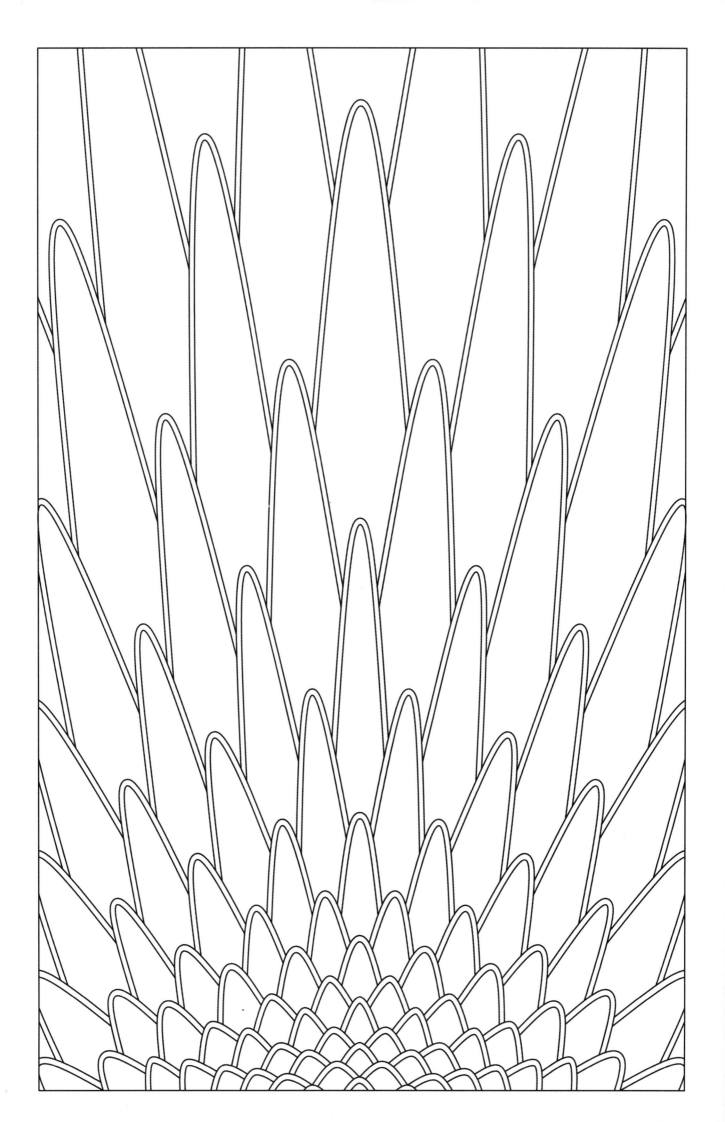

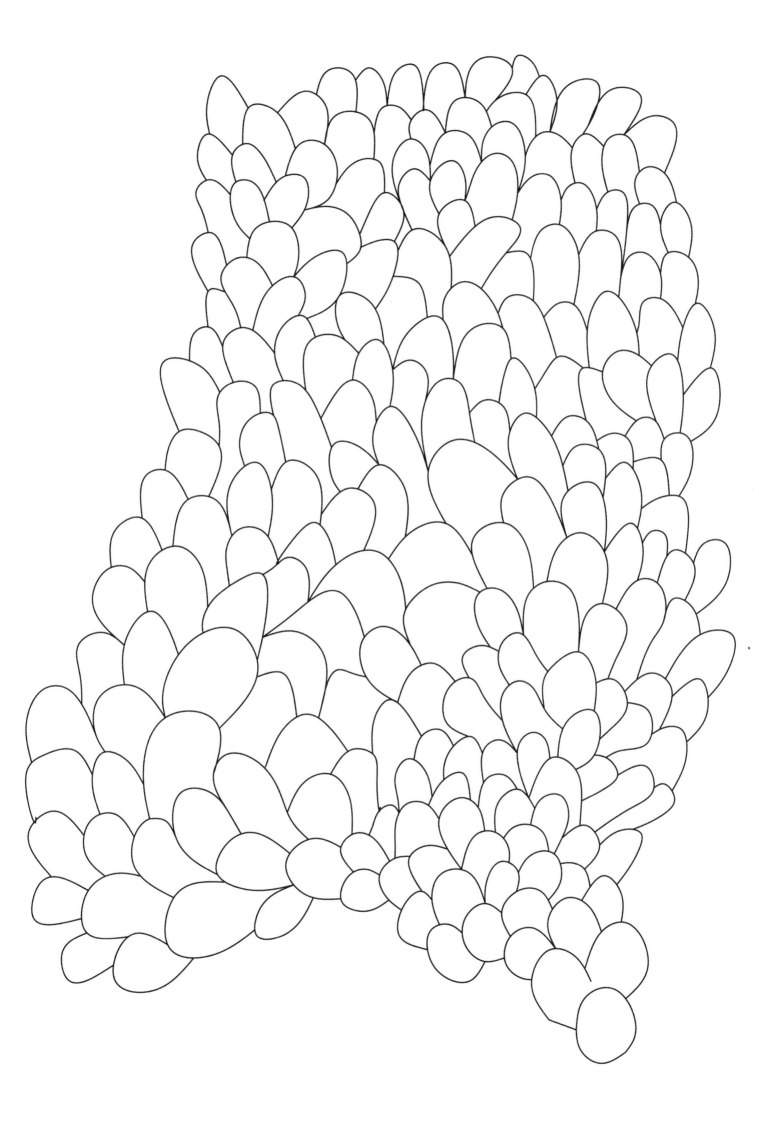

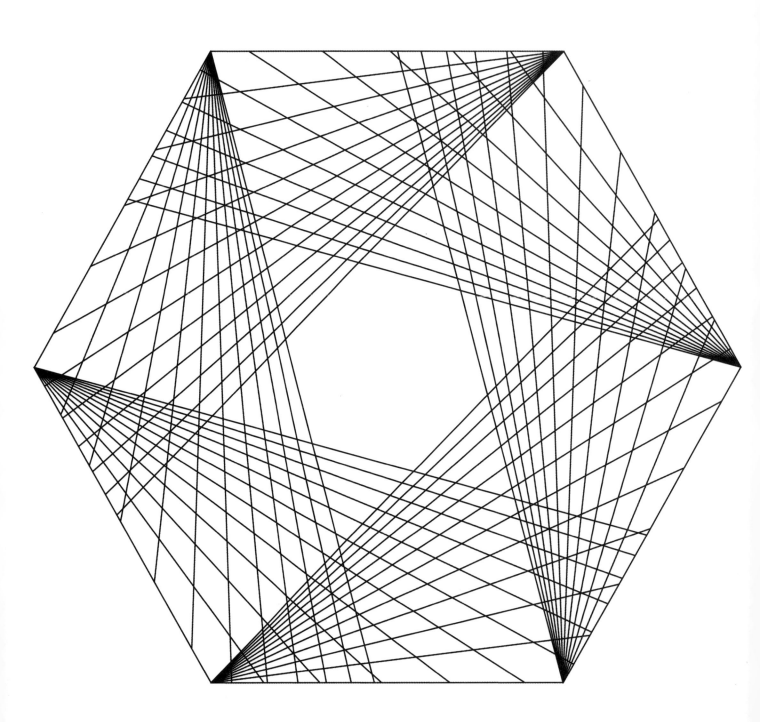

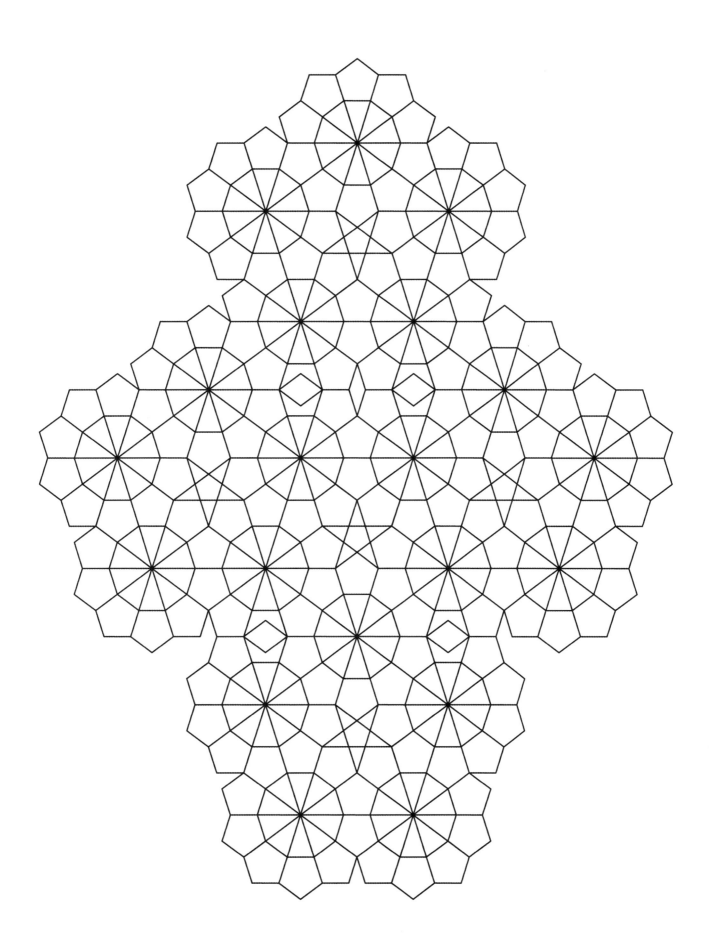

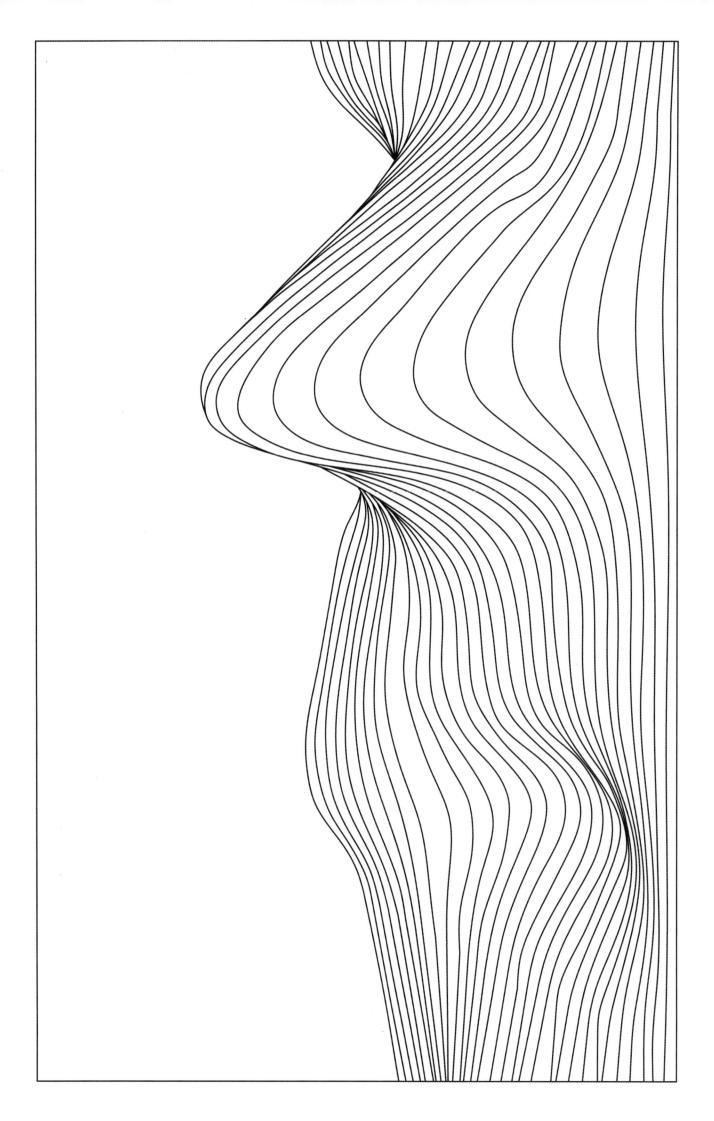

Published in 2016 by Hardie Grant Books

Hardie Grant Books (Australia)
Ground Floor, Building 1
658 Church Street
Richmond, Victoria 3121
www.hardiegrant.com.au

Hardie Grant Books (UK)
5th & 6th Floors
52–54 Southwark Street
London SE1 1UN
www.hardiegrant.co.uk

A Cataloguing-in-Publication entry is available from the catalogue of
the National Library of Australia at www.nla.gov.au
Modern Meditation: Coloring for focus and creativity
ISBN 9781743791899

Website: www.colourtation.com
Facebook: www.facebook.com/colourtation
Instagram: @colourtation

Cover, illustrations and text design by Jack Dowling
Printed in China by 1010 Printing International Limited